Out in the Wilderness

Margaret Evans

Out in the Wilderness

A mother comes to terms with her gay children.

ISBN: 978-1-508-59199-3

DEDICATION

I dedicate this book to all those lesbian, gay and bisexual
people, their parents and family members who have
shared with me their life stories.

An insightful account of a family going through the often painful process of learning to understand each other. I am sure that both parents and their gay daughters and sons will recognise and be able to identify with Hilda, Sue and Jack. It is a very human story.

Jenny Broughton MBE, President of FFLAG

Contents

Acknowledgements to:

Sue Johnson

Paul Evans

Gwyn Evans

Vera Vaughan

Pershore No. 8 Writing Group

Foreword

Parents who read this fictional tale will recognise some
of the facts, fantasies, fears, difficulties and joys of
having gay children. I feel privileged to know them and
to have heard their stories.

Chapter I – Encounter

Susan parked her bicycle in the piled leaves against the park railings. She carefully secured it with the D-lock she took from her pannier. She put the key in her pocket, rather than her backpack, so that she could make a quick get-away if the meeting became too difficult. The backpack was over her shoulders which were hunched in her yellow hi-viz jacket. Bunching her hands in her pockets against the chill mist, she walked purposefully towards the park pavilion café, Lakeside. The sooner she got this over with, the sooner she could carry on with her usual morning cycle ride.

Fran should be there by now: Susan had deliberately arrived late. They had met unexpectedly in the chemist last week, both staring at the same display of shampoos. Susan had recognised her childhood tormentor with no difficulty, despite the many years that had passed. Fran was obviously older, but still had that same distinctive large nose, beady eyes and way of craning her head forward. The short hair was dyed blonde and looked somehow wrong with the pale and creased skin. Susan would have moved quickly away from the shelf once she realised it was Fran, but Fran had spoken to her without looking up, as she would to a stranger,

'These prices are silly aren't they? You can get these shampoos for £1 at Pound Stretcher!'

She looked up just then and recognised Susan.

'Why, Sue!' she had exclaimed in the same grating voice Susan remembered, 'it is you isn't it? It must be ten years! How lovely to meet again.' She laughed, 'I didn't know you still lived in this one-horse town. We moved back only last month – been everywhere, done everything.'

Susan had muttered something and pasting on her false smile she had said pleasantly, 'Yes, it's Fran isn't it?'

Fran had insisted they meet for a coffee soon, and Susan had felt pressured to agree. After all, she told herself, it was twenty, not ten years on as Fran had suggested – she should be able to hold her own against her childhood bully by now.

So here she was, reluctantly stomping through the fallen leaves and across the soggy grass. She entered the steamy café and her glasses misted up immediately. She was aware the café was pretty full and then she heard

Fran from the table in the corner. 'Over here Sue!' She took off her glasses and wiped them with a grubby handkerchief, before waving to Fran and banging her feet on the doormat to remove most of the mud. She weaved her way across to the table where she removed her jacket and hung both that and the backpack on the wooden chair opposite Fran. The helmet went on the floor.

'You could get the coffees as you are on your feet', announced Fran as Susan was about to sit down, 'I'll have a large cappuccino please.'

Susan went obediently to the bar and queued, furious with herself for doing just as she was told. The waitress began to fill the mugs from the steaming machine and called over her shoulder,

'I'll bring them over to you love, as they're rather full – that's £5 please.'

Susan suddenly realised that her purse was in her backpack by the table. She thought fast.

'Sorry, I don't have my purse on me just now – my friend over there is paying.'

She smiled confidently at the girl whose face had dropped.

'Oh, OK – it's not usual but I'll bring them over and take the money then.'

Susan felt empowered and went back to the table.

'I explained that you would pay when she brings the coffees over,' she announced confidently, staring at Fran and daring her to challenge the statement. 'I didn't have my purse on me – it's in my backpack.'

Fran looked at her surprised, the lipsticked mouth pouting a little as she fumbled for her purse in her designer bag. Then, after a slightly uncomfortable pause she said,

'Well, what's your life like now?'

'Good! But you start,' smiled Susan.

The coffees arrived and Fran paid.

Fran talked effortlessly and Susan found her mind wandering. She contemplated the layout of the hexagonal café with its glass roof, as she drank her coffee. Who had designed this extraordinary building in the middle of a municipal park?

'Yes, Pete was the worst – the things he wanted me to do! You wouldn't believe it, you know. But then you have to please your man in that area don't you, or they find a newer model? Which was exactly what he did anyway! Only been together twelve months. But before that there was Gary who I met in Cyprus, and we had three children of course, which tied him down a bit. We were both working then. Now the kids have done very well …'

Fran prattled on, unaware that Susan's mind was elsewhere.

The stream of talk gave Susan the chance to down her coffee and, at a pause, she glanced down at a non-existent watch and stood up. She felt too impatient to waste another minute.

'Oh, you're not going yet are you?'

Fran looked up, surprised, caught mid-sentence. She watched Susan struggling into her jacket and backpack and shoving her hair with difficulty into the helmet.

'I must get going. People to see – things to do. Good to catch up again, Fran – and good luck with the next project.'

'Oh – well, all right, yes …' Fran said to the retreating back, 'Goodbye …'

She raised her voice as Susan moved off,

'You didn't say where you lived? And we haven't arranged another time!'

Susan didn't turn and was already stepping out into the sunshine. She chuckled to herself and walked back to her bike with a spring in her step. She had grown in confidence during her years as an accountant and was pleased with herself for not letting Fran take control and order her about, as she had when they were teenagers.

Fran knew nothing about her partner, as Susan had been less than forthcoming when Fran had pried, instead letting Fran do all the talking, which she had been only too willing to do. In the space of half an hour, Susan had learnt all about her school-friend's three deceitful husbands, her high-flying career in sales and her successful brood of brats.

Susan was well practised at evasion when talking about her own life and had volunteered very little. She saw no need to feed anyone's curiosity about her domestic set up, or listen to their assumptions. Recently some people were even rude enough to question the details of her sex life.

'Are you the man?'

She could always see the shocked reaction in a person's eyes. Even in the twenty-first century with more openness in society, people reacted with disapproval, incredulity, or disgust. She remembered how Hilda, her mother, had reacted to Jack. She had put off telling her about herself until last week, when she had sent a letter with the news.

She would tell Karen about her little encounter with Fran when she got home. Fran had been only too willing to do all the talking and, when she pried, Susan had told her nothing about her partner Karen, nor her son Tom.

So she and Karen would have a laugh over a film and a cuddle later this evening and forget people like Fran.

Chapter 2 – The Letter

I was getting my breakfast ready on a stormy Monday morning in February, before setting off for work at the Blue Cross charity shop. I had been expecting my 'Cat World' magazine for a few days, so I was surprised to see only a soggy letter on the mat. Through the porch window I could see the postman was enveloped in a plastic poncho that almost covered his face, though it gave him scant protection from the slanting rain.

The letter was obviously not a bill and, with a start of pleasure, I recognised the handwriting on the envelope as from my daughter. Would I have time to open it and read it before I went out? I couldn't wait and decided to open it straight away.

'Hilda, I've been trying to tell you this for some time, but you don't listen on the phone. I'm gay. I've left Dave and I live with my partner Karen and her son now. Susan.'

I stood stunned by the door. It seemed like hours passed while I stared at the typed words in disbelief.

Then I stumbled back into the kitchen where the kettle was whistling, and sat down heavily to read it again. Just the two sentences typed on paper that seemed too large for the few words, but not for their huge significance.

Susan always typed when it was something important that she wanted me to understand clearly – typing seemed to be more serious, carry more weight. Her handwriting in any case is a spidery scrawl, easy to misinterpret. Although I'm her mother she's called me by my name since she was 18. We communicate by letter as it is difficult by phone, but I hadn't heard from her for months.

Susan said I wouldn't listen on the phone, but more likely that she didn't want to hear my reaction to such news. And she never takes account of my slight deafness now I'm 62. I haven't seen her for so long and didn't even know that she had broken up with that layabout Dave. I wondered how long ago that had happened.

I stared at the storm outside, which had begun flashing and growling, and I felt angry and confused. It was all so unfair – why me? Why this? I knew no-one among my friends in this situation, or with whom I could share the shocking news. I felt I was in different world with unknown rules. I must have sat there for ages trying to make sense of it all, staring at the letter, until I scrunched it furiously into a ball and burst into tears.

Eventually I began to think more clearly. It must have been our fault. What had we as parents done wrong? I was baffled that this should happen twice in our family. I couldn't bring myself to think of the common word, used by everyone nowadays, but unheard of in my youth when such people were considered mentally deranged, or criminal. I shuddered to think of my children being like that and felt dizzy with shock and disgust. It seemed we were one of the 'pretended families' that Mrs. Thatcher had derided. I had agreed with her then. Now I made a cup of tea and took it into the lounge to sit by the window, my Blue Cross duties forgotten.

Eventually the storm died a little. The rain ceased to lash on the window, the sky cleared and the trees dripped heavily onto the lawn. A few goldfinches came out and were soon busy at the feeders hanging from the tree.

I heard the phone, but let it ring for ages before I stumbled to answer it.

'Hallo?' I said weakly.

'This is Caroline, Hilda. Where are you this morning? I'm waiting for you to arrive before I open up! Are you ill or something?'

The Blue Cross manager's voice was sharp.

I agreed that I was not at all well today; there was no

way I felt I could face the world after such devastating news.

What Susan said in the letter felt impossible, especially since she'd been with Dave for several years. They must have broken up some months ago. Yes, she and Dave had argued and fought, but who doesn't in a relationship? I remembered that she and Jack grew up with her father and me quarrelling most of the time. We should never have got together – he was ten years younger than me.

Thank God Martin wasn't around to hear all this from Susan, although I wondered in the back of my mind if he'd received a letter too. Still it probably wouldn't bother him, as he had no morals anyway. He'd gone off years ago when the children were teenagers, with that floozy who made eyes at him in the office and was almost young enough to be his daughter. He'd left me struggling with our unruly son Jack, and Susan, both of whom moved away and never bothered with me now.

I drifted in an angry sea of reminiscences for a while and then jerked back to the present as the cat meowed and clawed at the chair. Bold and black, Sooty had refused to go out earlier, because of the rain. I tried to discourage him from using the litter tray, but he had done so today and, even though it was in the porch, the living room stank. After he'd gone out, I sank back into my chair, with my cup of cold tea.

What was to be done? I mourned that I would never be a grandmother. All the other women I knew, from my work in the charity shop and those at church, had reached this stage long ago. It seemed they were busy minding toddler grandchildren most days of the week. I noticed that if I ever joined them for coffee, like if I saw them in the town café with someone else, they hurriedly put away the proud photos of their grandchildren. It seemed they kept them hidden from me – maybe they thought I'd contaminate them by having a gay son.

Did they know already about Susan? What would people say? They almost certainly knew about Jack, as he had been very brash in his life style. I'd found this somewhat embarrassing when he had lived at home, but pretended to ignore it all and treat him as if he were normal and was just a lad who went around with his mates. In any case I hadn't seen him since he had left twelve years ago after a row. But for me to have two such weird children seemed very unfair. I wouldn't be able to hold up my head in public again and people would point and laugh at me or, worse still, pity me.

I remember thinking when Jack was almost 15 and had first told me – 'coming out' as he called it – that he would grow out of such nonsense – it was a phase. But it seemed unlikely now he was aged 29. Susan was nearly

35 and now expected me to believe the impossible –
that she had a sudden change! It seemed more likely that
she was on the rebound after finishing with Dave and
therefore very confused. Someone had to put her
straight, and obviously that should be me, her mother.
This gay business is all nonsense I told myself.

I didn't know what else to think and reached for the
phone. Then I realised that Susan hadn't given me her
new phone number, or the address she had moved to.
Her old mobile number was unobtainable. There was
nothing at the top of the letter. What was this about? I
had no means by which to contact her in order to rail at
her. I began to weep bitterly again, out of self-pity and
helplessness. Time passed and the room grew colder.

Later that evening I steeled myself to phone Martin. I
called his landline as I don't have his mobile number.
That woman answered, so I gritted my teeth and said,

'Can I speak to my husband?'

I always refused to acknowledge he was no longer
that.

I could hear her draw breath before she said
unnecessarily, 'Who is it?' and then when I hissed, 'You
know!' she said in a business-like way, 'Oh, you mean
my partner, Martin. Yes, I'll see if he's available to speak
to you.'

I'm sure that I heard laughter in the background and there was a long pause before he came to the phone.

Martin sounded resigned and was obviously chewing when he barked, 'Yes?'

He was not even polite or interested enough to say 'Hallo, how are you?' I hadn't spoken to him for many years, as I had long ago given up berating him and asking him when he was going to come home. I swallowed my anger and hurt, but managed to whisper,

'Susan has written that she's living with another woman!'

'Oh that!' He sounded cheerfully dismissive, 'The girls told us a few days ago when they came for a meal. What's the problem then? Not as bad as when Jack came out surely!'

He laughed grimly, and I was sure we both remembered the icy atmosphere, the disbelief, the anger and shame we had felt then, not long before he had moved out.

I felt out in the wilderness, completely on my own. I put the phone down – he already knew and what was more, our daughter had been eating at their house with her girlfriend. It was unbearable; my heart thundered and my head buzzed. I sobbed, feeling doubly rejected.

Chapter 3 – Jack

I knew when I was young that I was gay, but I spent my youth in a gang of boys trying to be butch and masculine. I sang in the church choir until I was 12, but gave that up as sissy. I took up bell-ringing for a while. I was quite good at this: I've a good brain for remembering patterns and could memorise the tunes of the different methods.

I'd told mum when I was 14 that I was gay, and she told Dad. I felt I couldn't keep the secret any longer and I'd hoped she would understand and be supportive. I was so confused by the sexual attraction I felt to some other boys. She was shocked and furious at first. Then she'd said that I would grow out of it and I was not to mention it again as it upset her. Dad was just worried about AIDS and the fact that I might be picked on. Mum and Dad split up after that, which made me feel guilty. I left school at 16 and went to work in 'The Quiet Man' doing odd jobs, like moving the barrels of beer up from the cellar, wiping tables and things. I tried not to be openly gay. I had tattoos and drank with the lads in the village, joining in the banter with the girls, even had a few dates – that sort of thing.

Sue was always supportive, but I haven't seen her for a while; not since she got together with Dave, who I never liked.

Then the vicar contacted me after a few years. One of the other ex-choir guys, a bit older than me, was getting married in Canada. The vicar and I'd both been invited to the wedding and he suggested we go together. It seemed a good idea, as I hadn't travelled at all and my mother thought he would be a good minder for me. Little did she know! He actually propositioned me, both on the journey when he tried to sit with his hand on my knee, and later in the hotel in the Gents, where he actually lent across the stalls and stroked my bottom. I was totally shocked – he was forty years older than me, married with a daughter and a son around my age. His son Brad and I used to hang around together in the village.

I froze, 'No!'

He moved away when he realised I wasn't going to respond. He said not to tell anyone – particularly my mother. Well I wouldn't would I? I was disgusted with him, furious and ashamed. I'm sure Brad never knew he behaved like that. But I understand better now. His generation was more closeted: people thought being gay was a mental illness. There was no way at my age he could've come out as a gay man. He probably tried to fit in with everyone else and pretended to be straight. He may even have thought getting married would cure him. Or maybe he was Bi.

But I was left wondering how he knew I was gay and that worried me a bit. Was it that obvious? No, I reckoned my mother must've actually told him! She was besotted with the church and the vicar was always visiting for chats and tea. I used to go out when he arrived, as I didn't want to be got at for not singing in the choir anymore.

I feel angry with them all and try not to contact any of my family, though I see Dad from time to time in the pub near where they live. I moved away from home to the next town when I was 17. Steve, who was my boyfriend, became manager of 'The Knave of Hearts.' I worked behind the bar, washing up and cleaning, and stayed with Steve in his flat.

But things have changed now.

Chapter 4 – Susan

'Well, I wonder how she's taken the news. She should have got the letter by now.'

I was musing aloud to Karen as I gazed out of the window at Tom, who was kicking a ball around on the green across the road at the front of the house. He is eight now; adopted by Karen as a baby. He seems to like me well enough and it's such fun having a child around. It was getting colder and he would be in soon.

I chuckled mischievously then, thinking about Hilda and glanced over my shoulder at Karen who was curled up on the settee, crocheting, with her long blonde hair hanging down and hiding her face. There was always something in her hands that she was making: embroidery, tapestry, or knitting. She looked up, throwing her hair back as she spoke,

'Who? What letter? Oh yes, your mum.'

'Hilda, yes. She's so stuck in her ways – so very last century – and always so judgmental. She needed to be shaken up – challenged.'

Suddenly feeling angry, I turned fully and faced Karen. 'I won't give her the chance to have a go at me. She was horrible to Jack when he came out. No wonder he left home – and then Dad went because she was horrible to him. I haven't told her our address – or even my mobile.'

Karen sighed and carried on with her crochet. 'It's so different from when I came out. My mum was brill – no issues really. So long as I was happy and could be myself. And the guys next door were gay anyway.'

Karen's mum, Linda, had always babysat Tom when Karen went out. That's how we met, as she was out on her own in a garden centre, eyeing up the apple trees that we had now planted in the garden here.

Karen continued, 'But then your mum's older and I guess she must have learnt different things about gay people in her day.'

'Well yes, I suppose so – she's older than Dad. He left when we were teenagers.' I paused thoughtfully. 'And she had a hard time growing up. She was only 12 when her family had that accident. Her dad left them after that as he thought it had been his fault. I guess he felt guilty when he looked at Gran. We never met Gramps. Hilda never had any fun really I suppose, as she looked after Gran.'

'Well then, she wouldn't have met any gay people,' commented Karen.

'We both thought our parents split because of Jack. Mum blamed him too, I think. But I reckon it was her getting at Dad all the time before that. He didn't come home from work, and when he was home he just said nothing.'

I paused, remembering it well. 'I was quiet like that with Dave – always avoiding him.'

I shuddered then. I'd been with Dave for two years. I went and sat on the settee next to Karen, who put down her crochet. I stroked her hair, which was as soft as a cat's and smelt of lavender.

'I could never talk to Hilda – like you do with your mum – about school, or friends, or my job. She never listens. She's always right, and I'm always wrong!'

I was getting tearful and Karen put a comforting arm around me.

'Well, your Dad's different anyway,' she said eventually, and I remembered that Karen didn't have a Dad, as he'd died from cancer when she was little. I mopped my eyes with my sleeve and hugged her too, the crochet hooking us together.

We'd told Dad and Shelley together about us, over one of our regular meals with them. To be fair, Dad had certainly looked surprised when I told him I'd dumped Dave and was with Karen now.

He'd said, 'Well that's nice for you both. I thought you were just friends. I never liked Dave anyway. He never had a decent job and couldn't have supported you in hard times. Funny bloke. Well I hope you'll be happier now – you look happy enough with Karen.'

It didn't matter to him what gender my partner was, as long as we were happy. He's so much more broad-minded than Hilda. I guess he had to be, as he left her for Shelley and never looked back. Jack acted out his confusion at school as he was only 15 – not doing his exams and cheeking the teachers. He was bullied by other kids for a while when he was younger, but then he turned aggressive and went around with a group of rowdy boys in the village. But I had always liked Shelley, who I'd known for years, as she was Dad's secretary and quite near my age. I used to call into their office on my way home from school. She was cool and liked the same pop music as I did. She always dressed fashionably and listened to me properly when I talked to her about things.

Later that evening, when we'd told them about us and Dad was out of the room, Shelley confided privately that she'd had a fling with a girl before she met Dad. I was excited and pleased, as I knew then that she understood. I'd squeezed Karen's hand under the table and we'd all smiled at each other.

Now I turned excitedly to Karen, 'Did I tell you – Dad and Shelley are going to have a baby? A half-sister or brother for me!'

'No! When did they tell you that?' said Karen surprised. 'When's it due? He's a bit old isn't he?'

'He's a lot younger than Hilda,' I began, 'and Shelley's only 39 ...'

Tom clattered in just then,

'Mums, what's for dinner? I'm starving!'

So we left the conversation for another day, although I was bursting to tell Karen about my plans. I went into the kitchen to serve up Tom's favourite spaghetti bolognaise and Karen sent him to wash his hands.

I was really pleased, as this was the first time he'd called me Mum as well!

Chapter 5 – Shelley

I was peeling an onion and thinking about the situation. It was certainly unusual for both of their children to be gay, but there was nothing wrong in that. Times had changed.

I thought back to my childhood and when I was caught kissing and fondling a girl behind the bike sheds. My parents were summoned to school. It was explained to us all why I had to leave immediately, even before my A levels. The headmistress, Miss Bowes, with her grey hair scraped tight back in a bun that emphasised her frowning face, had said primly in her high-pitched voice,

'I recommend you take her to a psychiatrist to get this confusion in her sorted out before it goes any further. She certainly can't stay here and be a bad influence on the other girls. She is endangering them and bringing the school into disrepute.'

The journey home had been silent as my parents were obviously deeply shocked and, to be fair, so was I at the fact that I had to leave school so suddenly. They harangued me when we got home about how shockingly immoral homosexuality was; certainly a crime and probably a mental illness. Mother was crying and my father tight-lipped. Something would have to be done. They phoned the doctor immediately.

Well, I didn't think much of the psychiatrist I was referred to. He was a mean-looking man with a bristly beard, whose 'cure for my illness' as he put it, was to try to seduce me by putting his hand up my skirt and brushing against me as I went through the door. I left home then and decided to go and stay at my friend's house. Her parents were more enlightened. I went to work as a receptionist in the office where my friend's father worked, but I was furious for years about my cheated education.

I sighed, and tears from the onion rolled down my face, as I remembered the difficult time when even my grandparents and cousins shunned me. Eventually I'd discovered that men could be attractive too. Martin, at the office where I worked, was very special. He was tall, dark and handsome, as they say. He'd talked to me when his marriage was going wrong with that frigid woman. It wasn't long before things developed between us. We've been together for quite a few years now, but Hilda has never accepted it.

Later when the casserole was bubbling in the oven,

Martin came in and I asked,

'What did you think about Jack being gay when he came out?'

He hesitated and his brow creased for a moment, before he answered,

'I still worry about him getting AIDS. He was bullied at school too. But, you know, people can do what they like as long as it harms no-one else – and bedrooms are private places.'

I gave him a hug and I knew we would both be very different towards Sue and Karen. Different from how my parents and family had been to me.

Chapter 6 – Martin

As we lay in bed, I found myself reflecting on life with Hilda, which I hadn't thought about for years. It was because she had phoned and I could hear she was so upset. Shelley was still awake too, as we'd made the mistake of having coffee too near bedtime.

'You can't sleep either?' I whispered into her cockleshell ear. We always slept snuggled like spoons.

'No, I keep thinking about the girls,' she said.

'Me too.'

'What's it like having two gay children?'

I side-stepped the direct question and leant up on my elbow away from her. She had her face turned towards me and I could smell her lilac perfume.

'Well, we were both shocked when Jack came out, and we didn't deal with it at all well.'

Shelley listened as she always does and snuggled closer.

'But now I feel differently about the girls. As long as they're happy, that's all that matters.'

'What about grandchildren?' commented Shelley.

I sighed. 'I've no right to have grandchildren, nor to dictate how people live,'

I paused and added,

'But I do wonder if our marriage breakdown affected the kids more than I realised.'

I felt a quick surge of guilt, but Shelley expostulated,

'That's ridiculous! It's nothing to do with that. I can't believe that everyone with a bad marriage, or divorce, has gay children – don't be silly! Anyway Jack came out before you left Hilda.'

'Well then, perhaps it's more likely they were rebelling against their control freak of a mother.'

I paused again, thinking back to the way we'd argued over everything since the kids were born.

'Maybe I should've gone when they were toddlers.'

'I don't think it's the parenting. Lots of mothers or fathers are control freaks and they don't have gay kids. I think people are born gay,' said Shelley, 'Or bisexual,' she added. 'I expect it's genetic.'

I still felt after all these years that I had to justify why

I'd left Hilda, even though things had been awkward with Jack.

'You know, I just couldn't bear to be tied down anymore with things being so difficult – and when they were teenagers it all got too much.'

I didn't tell Shelley that I thought I deserved some teenage freedom, which I'd never had earlier in my life. My first girlfriend, Emily, got pregnant and I was pressured by my father and her parents to marry her, when I was too young. As fate decreed, once we had married, she lost the baby. Then tragically, she died herself not long after, with cancer. I was on the rebound, needing comfort after Emily had died so unexpectedly, so young. So I leaned on Hilda who lived next door, with her disabled mother. She'd seemed sympathetic. The age difference hadn't seemed to matter when I asked her to marry me, as she looked younger than her years in those days. I knew she wanted an escape from looking after her mother. I felt sorry for us both.

'After Hilda had our children, our sex life finished,' I continued. 'She just got more critical and nagging, like her mother. She'd have a go at me because I worked long hours and was tired at weekends. But one of us had to keep the wolf from the door.'

Shelley rolled over, away from me.

'It's difficult when you talk about Hilda,' she said. 'You were so unhappy. When you came into work you looked really down and stressed.'

I rolled after her and put my arm around her plump tummy. 'Any of my feelings for Hilda have long gone, Blossom: it's nearly 15 years now!' I whispered reassuringly.

Shelley had been the receptionist I'd known for years at work, who listened when I told her all my troubles. She gave me a reason to leave my marriage. I realised that I was happy now. I was looking forward to having our baby and the family I deserved. I still worked very hard at my job. They'd promoted me to Financial Controller, and I needed a woman to take care of me and to do all the chores.

I sighed as I snuggled down. Hilda was going to end up very lonely if she wasn't more accommodating to our children.

Chapter 7 – Exploration.

It was knowing that Shelley was pregnant which had got me thinking about having my own child. It was an exciting idea that had flashed through my mind after I heard the news, and had preoccupied me since. I liked Tom and knew I'd settled with Karen for keeps. I needed to Google more information and consult the lesbian chat rooms, but decided to talk to Karen the next day, after Tom had gone to bed.

She was 40, working as a secretary in the next town, and had chosen to adopt. With her long blonde hair and fine features, she certainly doesn't look the stereotype of a lesbian woman, which I probably do with my stocky build. Tom had been a few weeks old when Karen adopted him, and her mum had always been amazing.

I wanted to try for a baby of my own and wondered about a gay male donor, one who maybe wouldn't interfere too much in our lives together. I know such a thing is possible, but I was getting on at 35. It would take some planning and then I'd be old for having a baby. I started an internet search, while Tom was playing outside and the fish pie was cooking.

'Well, of course you need to think how your family and friends will react,' said Karen, later that evening, over the dishes. 'And how would you find a sperm donor who didn't want to be involved and who wouldn't complicate things with us?'

I scarcely heard her first comment, but replied to the second,

'Contracts can be drawn up and in fact many sperm donors don't want to be part of their child's life — although the child has the right nowadays to try and find their father when they are eighteen.'

I didn't tell her of the recent case where a sperm donor had changed his mind and won a court case to see his son.

I warmed to my subject and it all came out in a long discussion of the pros and cons. Karen bombarded me with questions,

'How will we manage financially when you give up work?'

But I had an answer for everything.

'Why would I give up work when I work from home?'

I audited people's small business accounts which they brought to me at home. I had my computer on a small desk in the spare bedroom, where Karen also kept all her fabrics, her wools and other craft materials.

'What if the baby came between us?'

'Why should it come between us anyway? Tom doesn't, does he?'

I'd done my research on the internet and knew about the recent laws, so I explained that a lesbian partner is allowed to be named as the other legal parent on the birth certificate.

'We'd need to be careful to screen for diseases or genetic disorders that a donor might have,' I continued, 'but there are agencies that deal with this, specifically directed at gay people as well.'

I got more excited and impassioned as I thought about it all, but that drained away in an instant when Karen asked drily,

'And your mother – Hilda? How will she react?'

I slumped at the table. How, indeed, would she react, given her strong moral and religious beliefs and refusal even to mention sex? I needed to think if indeed her reaction mattered to me at all, though I knew immediately that it did, from my feeling of dismay at the mere mention of her name.

Chapter 8 – Tom

Tom was careful not to let the other kids know he had two mums. He knew 'gay' was a term of abuse and had seen other children suffer and be bullied because of this. He was rather small for his age and had blond hair. He'd always been able to come home from school by himself as they lived only two doors away. No chance of his mums being discovered waiting at the school gates then! He'd always pretended he had a dad as, having been adopted as a baby by Karen, he could fantasize that he had the perfect father who worked away on an oil rig.

Sue, the new mum who had moved in a few months ago, worked from home and had begun to come to his school concerts and sports days. She seemed to like football. He pretended to the other kids that she was his other Gran, but not in her hearing of course, as he guessed she would have been furious. She was plumper and looked older than Mum. He didn't need to stay to the after-school club now Sue was living with them.

The kids at school knew Linda was his real Gran as

she'd always come to sports day, school concerts and plays. Mum was out at work and came home later. She took time off in order to be at parents' evenings, as she'd always done. He never asked friends round to play, just in case, but he played outside whenever he could, kicking a football around with whoever came out to play.

Tonight he was playing Monopoly with his mums. It was fun and he nearly always won! He knew there was something on their minds though, as they kept looking at each other – Mum looking worried, but Sue with a grin. He tried to keep the Monopoly game going past his bedtime by making his moves slow and thoughtful, but he knew this wouldn't wash if they had something to talk about.

'Right. Count up your money and your properties. Five minutes to bedtime, Tom,' said Karen briskly. He knew from her tone there was no point in arguing, so he sighed as he laid out his cards and money.

'Who's going to read me a story tonight then?'

He looked hopefully at Sue. He knew she didn't always know the rules and things might over-run if she read to him. Also she never made him read some of it first out loud to her, like Mum did.

'Well – let's add up our money first. Can you do

yours Tom? I have £4,552. And three sets of properties. How about you Sue?'

'Well mine's — let me see — £5,060, so more than yours. I have two sets of properties, and one station. I nearly had a hotel!'

Sue smiled and they both turned to Tom who was still fumbling the thin notes into piles and carefully spreading them out. He laboriously counted the thousands, then the hundreds, then the fifties and then the twenties, tens and ones, but the difficult bit was adding them up.

Eventually it was done, with both of them helping, and Tom was declared the winner.

As he lay in bed that evening, listening to his mums talking in the room below, he wondered what was going on.

He didn't think he was in trouble. They wouldn't have been playing with him otherwise. But he couldn't help worrying a bit as he turned off his light.

Chapter 9 – The Way Forward

The thought of my mother niggled away at me, but I had successfully put her to one side with my answer to Karen that evening, 'Well, I'll just have to write her another letter!'

I was wondering as I did the ironing one evening, about how Karen's friend Mary and her partner, Lisa, had managed to conceive Lisa's child, Olivia. She was a lively little girl, nine years old and with pale auburn curls.

'Let's have them round for a meal and a chat,' I suggested later to Karen as we snuggled up in bed. A full moon glinted through the half-drawn curtains, seeming to smile at us.

'If you like,' murmured Karen sleepily. 'But you'll have to do the cooking – I'm not for planning dinner parties – never had to do it.'

The following day Karen emailed Mary and it was arranged that they would come for Sunday lunch.

Later that Sunday, after roast chicken, we sat and drank raspberry tea. The two children were absorbed in a computer game in Tom's room, so I took a deep breath and asked my burning question:

'Tell us then, how you conceived Olivia.'

Lisa and Mary looked at each other and laughed. Lisa began explaining.

'Oh it was a game! But a bit embarrassing really. We advertised online for a gay donor to begin with, as they wouldn't allow lesbians to use IVF then.'

'Yes,' interrupted Mary, 'and we had three people respond!'

Lisa continued, 'so then we had to vet them, which was tricky. Like, what did they look like? Were they healthy? Did they have a disability? Did they have any other kids? Did they have a partner? If so, what did the partner think?'

'Why did they want to do this? And did they want, or expect contact with us all afterwards? And did we actually like any of them?' added Mary.

'Oh my goodness – a proper inquisition!' exclaimed Karen, squirming on the settee. 'I couldn't do that – too embarrassing!'

'Yes, but you've got to be sure they're all right if you

do it yourself. With IVF now they screen for diseases. It's all done in a lab. We didn't have that luxury,' said Lisa earnestly.

'And you want to be sure they're responsible people, work hard and so on,' added Mary. 'Would they want to put any money into it for us and the baby? I mean they might contribute some sort of child fund if, say, they wanted to have contact with the child.'

'So when you'd chosen your donor, what did you do then?'

Mary and Lisa looked at each other again and dissolved into fits of laughter.

'Well, we really wanted to make the baby by ourselves at home – not in his flat – but we weren't going to have him round, so we met in the Gay Jester and …'

Mary took over the explanation again.

'To cut a long story short, we had several attempts. It needs to be done quickly before the sperm dies. He had to perform into a jar, which we put under Lisa's arm to keep warm, whilst I drove home fast. Then we went to bed to make it romantic.'

'Yes,' continued Lisa, 'but it didn't work the first time. The sperm cooled too soon, so we had to go to his flat. We knew him a bit better by then. He took himself off into the bedroom and wanked off over a load of gay porn, before bringing out the result.'

'We then rushed off back home. We used a turkey baster, and the rest, as they say, is history.'

There was a pause and Mary added,

'We did wash the turkey baster!' and we all laughed.

Karen and I talked long into the night after our friends had gone. Could we use one of Jack's friends? I definitely knew I couldn't go about getting pregnant this way – too embarrassing. Mary's description of the break-neck car journeys with the precious liquid in a bottle under one arm put me off. It felt humiliating and bizarre. I knew the law had changed since their time, so I could go for IVF to a clinic, despite being lesbian.

We agonised about everything for a few weeks. I found out that as lesbians, we were eligible to use the NHS IUI scheme which would not be too expensive. What would the likely cost be at an agency? The internet suggested between £4,000 and £8,000, plus the cost of drugs – which were cheaper in Asda, it said! How would we afford this? It was the price of the new kitchen we had promised ourselves and no summer holiday with Tom. Would Dad, Martin, be willing to stump up the money for a potential grandchild? We went over all the possibilities we could think of, until at last Karen was on board. I'd start the ball rolling. I decided to contact the GoBaby agency. They did health checks on its sperm donors and assisted with artificial insemination. I'd also approach my doctor to see what the NHS offered.

We agreed on a termination if the child had a disability. I still remember my Gran, who had lived in the 'Futures' care home nearby. She had been moved in there once Hilda went to marry Dad. Gran had been mentally and physically disabled since my mother was young. I knew I couldn't do what Hilda had done. Being a young carer had made her an embittered person. Her father had gone and she'd been left as the sole carer for her mother, with no brothers or sisters to share the load. She'd made Dad's life a misery too, with all her demands on him. It was as if she thought he could make up for what she'd missed in her youth.

I hadn't realised that I still cared about what Hilda thought, but Karen's challenge to me that evening some time ago, had brought me up short. I really should go round and check on her. Try and see if we could build bridges. She must have read my letter by now – why hadn't she phoned? I'd forgotten I didn't give her my new number.

My view of Hilda was changing, as I recognised she must've had a difficult start to life. She certainly knew nothing about how the world had moved on, or how people in same-sex relationships were treated now. She wouldn't have known about the new laws in the 21st century.

Karen's mother, Linda, had explained how different the world was for their generation as they grew up. I'd shared with her my problem with Hilda, and was beginning to understand the challenges my mother faced.

Chapter 10 – The Vicar Drops In

I'd stopped going to church. I felt confused and ashamed. When Sandra called round to ask about the flower rota, I barely spoke to her and closed the door quickly.

'I should think the whole village will be talking behind my back and pitying me,' I thought. 'How could God do this to me anyway? It's not fair.' I felt sure that same-sex relationships were rightly condemned, both in the Bible and by the Church, so I was condemned for giving birth to two such freaks of nature – my children.

I took to going to the supermarket in the next town to avoid people. I never went to do my turn on the rota at the Blue Cross like I was supposed to. I phoned each week and said I was ill. No-one liked me there anyway – I could tell. Someone had the cheek to tell me I should smile more and why didn't I rinse my hair? I felt like a frump with my stern face. I can see in the mirror that I have a frown, and my mouth turns down at the corners.

'This is what caring for my family has done for me', I

thought. I'd put on weight after the menopause, but not as much as some other women in the village. Thinking of them made me pull a wry face, as I remembered they were all grandmothers now. I wasn't, nor was I likely to be after this recent news. Well I wouldn't care about the family anymore, as it was evident that I was no good at it and had totally failed as a parent.

I was surprised and flustered therefore, to open the door to the vicar, five weeks after I had received Sue's letter. Reverend Luke invited himself in, so I had to reluctantly open the door wider and offer him a chair and a cup of tea.

I clattered a lot in the kitchen, moving unwashed pots and pans to get to the kettle and find some clean china. I tried to compose in my mind what I would say.

Luke sat down in the chintz armchair by the window and I could see him through the hatch from the kitchen, looking out at the unfilled bird-feeders in the garden. Sooty meowed and jumped on his lap, purring loudly. It was a while since the cat had jumped on me and, as I came back into the room, my eyes filled with tears at another betrayal from my pet.

'Hilda, you don't seem to be yourself. We're all concerned as we've missed you in church for several weeks,' commented the vicar, as he took the cup from me. 'I was wondering if you were all right and if the family were well.'

He looked around the dusty room. I'd rather given up on myself and the housekeeping since I'd received the letter. I'd allowed clutter to intrude into my usually neat living room. There were unwashed cups and saucers on every available surface, which was most unlike me. I noticed Luke had wrinkled his nose as he passed the dirty cat litter tray in the porch.

'How is Susan getting on?' he continued, as I said nothing. I burst into tears.

'Oh Luke, I can't believe it, but I expect you and the whole village know. Susan's split up with Dave and … and … she's living with a woman!'

The vicar drained his cup of tea and waited quietly until I'd dried my eyes and composed myself.

'Hilda,' he said gently, 'there's nothing wrong with that. Susan is an adult.'

'You don't understand – she says she's gay too! And I won't be a grandmother now will I? And … and I feel so weird having two gay children!'

I'd confided in the previous vicar shortly after Jack had come out, and when Martin left. He had children of his own and understood, but this new vicar was younger and unmarried. What did he know about life?

'We don't know yet whether or not you will be a grandparent,' Luke said gently. 'How is Susan getting on in the new relationship – has she told you?'

'She hasn't been back to see me. I don't know where she is. She just sent me this letter. What am I to do? No-one cares about me.' I pursed my lips and continued bitterly, 'It's all because of Martin, I'm sure. He was a useless father!'

'Now Hilda, you are not to blame yourself, nor their father. You know, being gay, although in a minority, is part of the normal range of sexuality. We know that now from scientific studies.' He paused, 'And of course there are homosexual creatures in the animal kingdom.'

I stared at him in disbelief.

'What? You think it's nothing to do with me or Martin?'

'Probably not,' asserted the vicar. 'Your children have been very brave to tell you, I think. Life's very difficult for gay people. They are labelled and condemned unnecessarily.'

He paused and looked at his empty tea-cup, as I stared at him surprised.

'It's not as bad as when you were young of course – I mean younger. Then, as I expect you remember, people were put in prison for being gay. Criminalised.

Remember, Oscar Wilde was imprisoned?'

I shook my head, still trying to get my thoughts round his accepting attitude.

'Had you heard of him – Wilde?'

I shook my head again.

'Alan Turing was another,' Luke continued, 'the man who broke the enigma code in the war. He was criminalised for being gay. They forced him to take a female hormone. He was unable to continue working for GCHQ as gay men were thought to be a security risk. Then he committed suicide. Shocking!'

He paused again and shook his head before continuing,

'Yes, people even had electroconvulsive therapy to 'cure' them, as it was thought of as a mental illness.'

'Yes, I do remember that,' I interjected. 'We had a man in the village who changed completely after he'd been to hospital. We kids all avoided him then. Though he'd been fun with us before that – he always listened to us and let us play in his garden. Some of the other parents didn't like their children talking to him though. I expect they thought he was a paedophile – which he wasn't,' I added hastily, 'but my mum never knew that I spoke to him of course. He was very understanding before he went to hospital – I bet he had that therapy.'

There was a pause, as I was remembering my childhood and the supportive adults that had been around when I was caring for my disabled mum. Luke, who had only been in the parish a few months, did not know about my earlier life. He seemed to know that my son was gay, but everyone seemed to know that in the village. All that gossip.

'But what about the Bible?' I wailed again. 'I am sure it says it's wrong and they will go to Hell!'

'Wherever did you get that idea?' Luke said gently. 'Yes, there are fundamentalists who would condemn same-sex behaviours as unnatural. But they have not researched the Biblical texts that appear to condemn male homosexuality. Many of the words have been mistranslated. When they were written, the Jews were being urged to have more children. And lesbianism isn't mentioned at all.'

The vicar was obviously warming to his theme, which was such an eye-opener to me.

'And moreover the one story that gets trotted out by the homophobes is actually a story about inhospitality to strangers and there's much dispute about the translation of the original words. Scholars say there are inaccurate translations in many places. There's a lot written that could counter some of those arguments. The people who wrote the Biblical texts had a limited understanding of homosexuality. They didn't think about committed same-sex relationships that we know exist nowadays. They were referring to temple prostitution, or casual sex.' He smiled and paused. 'I could go on, but how about another cup of tea?'

I got up, my mind racing, and went back into the kitchen to re-boil the kettle. I was already beginning to feel a great weight lifting from my mind. The vicar seemed to know a lot about the subject and wasn't blaming me.

When I returned with the teapot, I saw that he'd taken my Bible off the shelf by the window. He was smiling as he flicked through the pages. He continued in his slow drawl, as if he was enjoying the opportunity of preaching a sermon to an unbeliever.

'Most people like to look instead at the bright stories of David and Jonathan, or Ruth and Naomi. The Bible is not a book to beat people with – it's poetry and storytelling, not hard unyielding doctrine. Jesus put people before dogma. He never mentioned homosexuality at all! He showed us a God who never chooses one person at the expense of another. The Bible should be a tool of liberation and sensitive mission, about a God who is inclusive ...'

He stopped and smiled at me. I was gazing open-mouthed at all this.

'How do you feel now Hilda? Will we see you in church again?'

I was not sure. I needed time to think things through.

Chapter II – The Manager

Two days after the vicar's visit, the Manager of the Blue Cross, Caroline, turned up unexpectedly on Hilda's doorstep. She was a tall statuesque woman who stood no nonsense from her employees, even though many were volunteers. If Hilda was ill, unusually for her, well then she needed to make a sick visit and had brought some flowers. She both rang the bell and rapped the brass knocker peremptorily. Hilda started when she saw who it was through the porch window.

She opened the door rather gingerly, guiltily aware she was off work for something other than her stated reason.

'Hilda, my dear, we've missed you at the shop,' said Caroline in a treacly voice. 'Whatever is the matter? I hope it's not serious. Have you been to the doctor? Here, I brought you some flowers.' She thrust the budding daffodils into Hilda's hand.

Hilda stepped back and the woman came in.

'Er ... no. It isn't serious really,'

Hilda began and then burst into tears as she turned to go into the kitchen.

'I really can't tell you, it's all so awful! I'm not ill. I'm just very shocked and upset.'

Caroline was exasperated, but also concerned. Hilda was a reliable volunteer who she couldn't do without in the shop, even if she only came in three days a week. She was known for being severe and punctilious and the younger employees usually behaved better around her, although she was not liked for her sharpness.

Caroline plonked down on one of the wooden chairs.

'Now I'm sure it can't be as bad as all that. Tell me! Is the family all well – how are your children? You do have children don't you?'

Hilda sat down on the other chair, abandoning her task of putting the flowers in water and sobbed even louder.

'You won't understand, but Susan has another partner and, I can hardly say the word, but she ... she's with a woman!'

Caroline visibly relaxed. 'Oh, is that all? You mean she's gay? I don't understand. What's the problem then?'

Hilda stared at her in surprise, wiping her eyes and

then wailed,

'You don't think that's bad then? I can't believe it –
my family is ruined and I'll never be able to hold my
head up again. My son's gay too! I'll be a laughing
stock.'

'Come, come,' soothed Caroline, patting her hand.
'That is just nonsense Hilda dear. My nephew is gay and
he's a barrister now! I also have a lesbian aunt on the
other side of the family. It's no problem. I'm sure your
children are delightful people. Then the Patels at the
One-stop shop have a gay son too. He works very hard
and is a lovely man. I'd thought one of you must have
cancer, or something terrible happened. Now pull
yourself together. I want you back at the shop by
Wednesday.'

With that she scraped back her chair and marched
out of the front door. She couldn't waste her free
afternoon on such ridiculous matters and she rather
regretted the money spent on the daffodils.

Chapter 12 – Susan and Hilda

Susan arrived unexpectedly at her mother's house two weeks later. She was surprised to see that Hilda was looking less stressed than usual, wearing a fresh blouse and skirt and she appeared pleased to see her, giving her daughter a little peck on the cheek. Things had improved since the vicar's visit but Susan didn't know about this. So she didn't see the disarray that had been in the house after the sudden arrival of her letter, as Hilda had set to and cleared up the mess. The litter tray had gone from the porch. Sooty who had been outside, pushed past her to get in from the cold, meowing reprovingly and piteously.

Susan followed her mother cautiously into the kitchen. Hilda put the kettle on.

'Well, it is nice to see you dear,' said her mother, somewhat formally. 'Are you keeping well? I haven't seen you for quite a while now.'

'Hilda,' began Susan slowly, looking at her mother's back with its short straight grey hair. 'We need to talk.'

She paused, as Hilda said nothing but continued with the tea things, her back still firmly turned.

'How have you been recently, since I,' she hesitated, 'Since I told you about me and Karen?'

Hilda turned and faced her, taking a deep breath. 'Well I must admit I was surprised, especially after Dave – not that I liked him particularly,' she added quickly. 'And I thought probably you were confused and on the rebound.'

Her tone was not at all what Susan had expected, but calmly angry and restrained, unlike the high-pitched hectoring she was used to from her mother.

They went into the sitting room carrying the tea mugs, and sat facing each other at the old oak dining table against the far wall.

'No mum. I think I've always been gay – Dave and I used to argue about sex all the time – and I hated it.' She shuddered with the memory. 'I feel so much happier now. Meeting Karen was the best thing that happened to me. It gave me the push I needed to move out from Dave's.' She paused, 'I know he was upset – and I can see you were too.'

Hilda's eyes had filled with tears, but Susan could not know how her hopes of a grand wedding for her daughter had been dashed, along with her hopes of future grandchildren. Hilda's pain was almost unbearable.

'It wasn't fair on either of us. We weren't happy and I wasn't being honest with myself,' Susan continued. 'He's found another girl now who will make him much happier.'

Hilda blew her nose loudly.

'I had to write the letter. You wouldn't have understood. I didn't think I could say it to your face. But I can now. I'm gay. It's a relief to be myself – gay.'

She stopped and looked at her mother who had winced at the word and whose face was now working with emotion.

'I know you were upset with Jack, but we can't be any different, he and I. We are who we are and being gay is not the sum of who we are. We are the same people we were before, you know!'

There was a pause, then she added quietly, 'and Dad is all right about it.'

She looked quickly at her mother, as it had never been permitted for her, or Jack, to mention their Dad Martin at all to Hilda since he had left.

Hilda stiffened and bit back with her automatic response, 'Well he would be wouldn't he? No morals!'

In the long silence that followed, she squashed down in the corner of her mind how difficult it was for Susan to hear her father criticised. There was also the implied criticism of Susan's morals. It would not have occurred to her before, but she had done a lot of thinking since the vicar's visit and he had challenged her in many ways, including the tone of voice she used when upset.

'Yes, well,' she said gruffly instead, and looked closely at Susan. She was the same daughter after all – nothing had changed – just her choice of partner. She still had the tousled dark hair similar to her own and the short stocky build that Hilda had herself when younger. Everyone had said Susan looked like her mother, with the pointed nose and thin lips.

'Well, where're you living now?' Hilda continued.

'It's a lovely terraced cottage, next-but-one to the school in the village over the hill. Karen, my partner has a son Tom, who she adopted as a baby. He likes football.'

In her surprise, Hilda couldn't help blurting out,

'But I didn't think people, like you,' she emphasised the words, feeling unable suddenly to say the word gay, 'Could have children, or adopt! Bad influence you know.'

She wished she hadn't said this as soon as the words

were out of her mouth. She didn't know how to apologise however, as she had never done so to anyone in her life before. Susan, she noticed, coloured with annoyance and gritted her teeth, but continued drinking her tea. She was reiterating to herself that Hilda's generation had grown up with a set of false beliefs and faulty understanding about such issues. Karen's mother, Linda, had put her wise to that, and had explained how difficult she had initially found understanding Karen when she'd first come out. So Susan did not leave the table as she would have done in the past but, after another heavy pause, said instead,

'Mum, would you like to talk to Karen's mother about how it was for her when Karen came out?'

Hilda squirmed and hesitated. The thought of telling anyone else seemed impossible, but then this lady would have been through similar emotions perhaps, and just might understand. Also she would be unlikely to tell anyone else, as she had a daughter 'like that' herself. Hilda stood up and moved slowly over to the window, gazing at the chaffinches scrabbling around under the tree. The starlings were bullies and kept moving them busily out of the way.

'I don't know, I might,' she conceded, hesitantly and Sue, watching her closely, breathed a sigh of relief.

'I know!' she said brightly.' How about I invite you

round for a cup of tea one Saturday?'

'But … but,' protested Hilda, 'I haven't even met your friend yet! She might not want me round to tea.' She could not even bring herself to say Karen's name and suddenly felt shy and embarrassed.

'Of course she'll want to meet you and so will her mum – and Tom of course.' She drained her tea, stood up briskly and strode into the hall to get her anorak and bag.

'Right, let's say next Saturday – I'll come and pick you up around 3 o'clock, so be ready.'

Hilda, speechless, had trotted after her into the hall. She was surprised when Susan gave her a big kiss, before swirling out of the door and down the path to her little yellow Renault, calling over her shoulder,

'I'm so glad we can talk to each other again, Mum.'

Overwhelmed, Hilda sat down on the hall floor – holding her spinning head in her hands. But as she sat there confused, she realised she also felt a tremendous relief that Susan had made contact again. She struggled with her conflicting feelings, still wanting to blame someone or something. Sooty rubbed himself against her shoulder and put his face in hers.

And it was only later as she cried herself to sleep, that she realised she still didn't have any address or phone number for her daughter, so she would have to be ready for her on Saturday at 3 o'clock. She had no idea how old Karen or her mum were, nor for that matter this child Tom.

Undoubtedly she would need to look her best, though that was far from how she felt about the whole situation.

Chapter 13 – The Visit.

The following Saturday arrived sunny but cold. Hilda had been uncertain what to wear, surprised at the turmoil in her mind. She was usually quite decisive. Eventually she chose her calf length blue spotted skirt from Marks and Spencer and a raspberry coloured velour roll neck pullover, with a navy jacket on top. She was a mixture of emotions, both excitement at seeing where Susan lived and trepidation at wondering what her partner was like. She had forgotten temporarily the woman's mother was also to be there, and Susan had not given her any name.

Then she wondered about the little boy whose age she was uncertain of. She had decided to take him a toy car as a gift. She found one which had been Jack's – a red sports car – as she didn't like to arrive empty-handed and couldn't face the questioning looks at the village shop if she bought anything else. She was feeling very anxious and unsure how she should behave.

Susan's car horn pipped and her mother let herself

out of the front door, locking it carefully behind her. Sue watched her wobble down the path on her high heels; pleased to see her mother had made an effort with her appearance. She always carried her chin up – a consequence of being short – but this rather gave her the appearance of having a bad smell under her sharp nose.

As she walked down the path Hilda supposed she would sit in the back of the car, as she could see her daughter's friend was in the front seat. However Karen jumped out as soon as Hilda approached and came towards her, face beaming. She had long blonde hair and was dressed attractively in jeans and a green roll-neck pullover. Hilda could see she was taller and slimmer than Susan. She held out a hand, which Hilda took uncertainly.

'Hallo Sue's mum, I'm Karen. Pleased to meet you,' she enthused. She continued brightly. 'What should I call you?'

Hilda hesitated, a bit taken aback.

'Mrs. Stone,' she said rather primly.

'Well Mrs Stone, do sit in the front,' and Karen held the door open for her, smiling.

Hilda felt somewhat disarmed, but smiled formally and got in. And without more ado Karen squeezed her lanky frame into the back seat. It was all very clean and tidy. Sue's eyes caught Karen's in the mirror and they set off towards their home. Karen leaned forward over Hilda's shoulder as Sue revved the engine and drove off. She continued in a chatty tone,

'Mrs. Stone, Sue said it would be nice for you to meet my mum. I'm collecting her and Tom from football shortly and she will join us for a cup of tea.'

'Oh yes!' said Hilda uncertainly. 'And what should I call your mother?'

'Her name's Linda,' said Karen, still smiling.

'Oh well then, I had better be Hilda to you all,' said Hilda, relaxing a bit.

Sue smiled in the mirror and stepped on the accelerator.

'I never thought to ask you where you lived,' began Hilda.

'Oh, you'll see soon enough,' laughed Sue. Hilda had never seen her daughter so energised and happy.

'It's a rented cottage just two doors down from Tom's primary school. He's playing football this afternoon in Bromsgrove, so Karen will fetch him and her mum at about half past three.'

Hilda relaxed a bit as she thought she would have Susan to herself while Karen was out. Karen and Sue chattered away in the car about their bathroom, which the landlord was going to have renovated. It didn't seem to matter that Hilda was there, saying nothing.

Presently they arrived at an attractive terrace of small houses, just before the town began and opposite a playing field which evidently belonged to the nearby school. Theirs was the second in a row of similar red-brick houses, dating from Victorian times, next-door-but-one from the school. The primary school was a rather severe-looking Victorian building with tall windows too high for any child to see out.

Hilda was shown through the green front door which led directly into the living room, just past a small area for hanging coats and depositing shoes. The young women hurried into the kitchen and busied themselves making tea. Hilda was glad to be left on her own for a while to take in her surroundings.

The natural wood floor was mostly uncarpeted, but there was a long brown hessian rug in the middle. On that stood a low white table. Hilda stood and looked towards the window, through which she could see a substantial hawthorn tree with a light green haze of early spring leaves. The leaves seemed to flow into the room, cascading down the cushions on the low green settee which seemed to invite her to sit. Instead, she walked carefully round the table and sat on the single wing-backed chair upholstered in white with a continued leaf motif. A green shawl was flung carelessly over the seat. She picked it up and examined the neat shell crocheting. In the corner of the room was a tall bookcase with a chirpy wooden blackbird on top. A vase of ivy stood on one of the shelves and there was a picture of a young boy in school uniform smiling at her. An owl piggy bank was next to the photo on a pile of telephone directories. On one pale wall to the right of her, was a tall picture of a silver birch. The white trunk was painted on the pale green speckled ground, with yellow light shining through the trees beyond. A white standard lamp stood in one corner, its shade slightly askew.

The whole atmosphere in the room was one of peace and light. It felt as if spring was in the room itself and Hilda felt her heart lighten.

Susan came in with the tea tray and placed it on the table, followed by Karen with a silver teapot and a plate of fairy cakes. Hilda felt like the queen.

'It's a lovely room,' commented Hilda, as she took the proffered cup and a cake. 'So how long have you lived here Karen?'

'Oh, for three years,' responded Karen. 'I lived with my mum when Tom was a baby, but when he started school I rented this place as it's so convenient.' She spoke with a soft Worcestershire drawl.

'Did you do this?' asked Hilda, indicating the crocheted shawl across her knees.

'Oh yes,' said Karen. 'I love working with wool and doing embroidery. Anything like that really. Mum taught me. She's good like that.'

She and Sue sat down together on the settee.

Hilda looked at them and asked tentatively. 'So where did you meet each other then?'

The young women laughed and said together, 'online – a dating agency!'

Sue then had to explain this to her mother who did not use a computer. Hilda was taken aback at this novel way of finding a partner.

'Then we arranged to meet up at the garden centre.'

'Oh goodness, look at the time! I have to fetch Tom and Mum from football. Excuse me!' and Karen jumped up, rushing to put on her coat and grab the car keys from the hook by the door. See you soon,' she called over her shoulder, banging the front door behind her.

Sue and Hilda were left alone sipping their tea. Hilda looked at her daughter, anxious at the thought of meeting the other mother, but said nothing. There was no way she could escape as Karen had taken the car.

'Well, what do you think of the house?' said Sue.

'I like it very much,' said her mother, gently playing with the shawl. 'She's a clever girl isn't she, Karen? Attractive looking too. Seems strange that she doesn't have a husband.'

Sue sighed despairingly and leaned forward staring at her mother.

'Hilda, she's gay like me!' she said emphatically, running her fingers through her hair.

Her mother shrank back, her mouth working.

'I just don't understand!' she wailed.

Suddenly there was a commotion at the front door, breaking the silence which followed her remark. Tom burst in, closely followed by Karen and Karen's mother, carrying his coat and football boots. The boy from the photo, aged about eight, stared briefly at Hilda, before turning his attention to his mother and saying in some surprise,

'Gosh, the room's tidy! What's to eat?' Without waiting for a response he took a cake.

Hilda smiled and Karen's mother deposited the boots and coat by the door before moving forward, her hand outstretched.

'You must be Sue's mum – I can see the likeness,' she laughed. 'I'm Linda.'

Hilda flushed, slightly embarrassed, 'Yes, people say she's like me – I'm Hilda. Karen doesn't look like you though!'

Linda was short like herself and with dark-grey bobbed hair.

'No, she takes after her Dad. Tall and handsome,' Linda laughed.

Hilda fished in her jacket pocket for the little car. 'Here, Tom, this is for you,' she said, holding it out for him. 'It used to belong to Jack, Susan's brother.'

Tom took the red car and examined it closely. 'Thank you,' he said shyly, but Hilda could tell by their smiles that Sue and Karen were both pleased that she had thought to bring a gift for the child.

Linda beamed at Tom and then turned to Hilda, 'Your Sue is a clever girl isn't she? All those accounts she does! Me, I can't add up. She's a good cook too. She made Tom a wonderful birthday cake when he was eight, didn't she Tom?'

He smiled shyly.

'Shaped like a car!' She helped herself to one of the cakes. 'Did you teach her that?'

Hilda was surprised, as she hadn't ever thought of Susan as clever, or as a good cook. She realised that she had thought of nothing but feeling sorry for herself since Susan had come out. She had also only focussed on her daughter's love life and sexuality, as if that was the sum of all she was.

'Er ... well ... yes, we did do a lot of cooking when she was younger,' she conceded. 'I don't know about recently, as I haven't seen much of her since she went to live with Dave, and now ...'

'Yes, she's moved in with Karen, which is lovely for both of them,' Linda finished her sentence. 'Karen doesn't cook much and has such a lot to do what with her work and Tom growing up. Boys eat like horses!' She laughed as Tom took another cake, and Hilda smiled, remembering Jack's voracious appetite.

Sue vanished into the kitchen to make fresh tea and Karen busied herself sorting Tom's boots and football kit.

'You must have a bath Tom,' she called after the clatter of noisy feet on the stairs.

'Karen told me that you were a bit shocked at Sue's news. I was at first with Karen,' said Linda comfortably. 'How about we meet up one day away from these two and have a cuppa and a chat?'

Hilda found herself agreeing. The conversation turned to Tom's football prowess, the car abandoned on the table.

Linda did not let the offer drop and pressed her to a date, so they had a firm arrangement before Hilda thanked them for the tea and said she must be going.

Sue ran her back home. Hilda was silent, her thoughts racing, but Sue knew she was processing all that happened and felt secretly pleased that her mother seemed to be open to change at last.

Chapter 14 – The Meeting

Hilda felt apprehensive, but excited as well. She wanted to talk honestly about her feelings and might unburden herself to Karen's mother Linda. They had agreed to meet on a certain bench in the grounds of Hanbury Hall, as they were both members of the National Trust and could get in free. Hilda arrived early and walked the little distance from the car park. She had brought a thermos flask of coffee and two mugs in a bag, as they had decided not to go into the tea shop, but to sit in the grounds of the big house for more privacy. It was a variable spring, but they hoped the weather would last and be warm enough to sit outside in the enclosed parterre garden. The house was not open, as it was not yet April, but people could wander in the grounds.

Hilda remembered bringing her mother here in her wheelchair many years ago, wheeling her up the tarmac path, together with her own small children. Jack had seemed a normal lad then, brandishing a cardboard sword and pretending to be a knight. Sue had agreed somewhat reluctantly to be a princess, wanting to be rescued. Maybe the warning signs were there then, she thought.

There were few tourists around today, as it was only just 11 o'clock and was not yet school holidays. She walked around past the orangery whose dirty windows caught the low sunshine. A few early daffodils were pushing up through the grass in a sheltered corner. They were nodding their heads in the breeze and looked ready to burst.

Hilda sat on one of the wooden benches placed around the square with their backs to the high hedge. The geometric borders were quite bare, freshly dug, with the low hedges neatly clipped. The miniature conical conifers made a pleasing design. A breeze stirred her straight grey hair and she lifted her face to the growing warmth of the sun, eyes closed for a moment. When she opened them she saw Linda, entering the garden between the tall brick pillars, leaning heavily on a stick and looking around for her.

Hilda felt suddenly shy, shivered and wondered why she had come.

Linda looked at the forlorn figure sitting on the bench and smiled. She remembered how surprised she had been when Karen came out, but knew that it made no difference to her feelings for her daughter.

'Well I'm glad the weather held,' she announced as she walked over to join her. 'I hope you haven't been waiting too long?'

Hilda got out the mugs and poured hot coffee from the flask. Both women sat and clasped their hands around the warm mugs, their breath mingling with the steam like mist in the cool air.

'Well, I bet you thought it was your fault didn't you? The only mum in the village with gay children?' began Linda, getting to the point straight away. The chill was beginning to get to her bones, and Hilda had said nothing.

Hilda laughed hollowly.

'Yes indeed, and what did I do wrong?'

'Well, we are brought up with everyone behaving in certain ways, according to whether they are men or women. We see this as normal and acceptable,' Linda sighed, adding, 'You expect everyone to grow up, get married to the opposite sex, and have kids. But some people aren't attracted to the opposite sex, but their own. Some even to both if they are bisexual. We're all different sexually, and probably on a spectrum from gay to straight.'

Hilda looked surprised at this mother's acceptance

and obvious knowledge about the subject. She remembered that the vicar had mentioned the range of sexuality too.

'What did you do as a job?' she asked.

'Oh me – I was a nurse. I met all sorts of different people, gay and straight, so it wasn't such a shock to me as to you, I guess. I had already thought when Karen was quite young that she might be gay. Though it's not what I really expected. But when I was growing up, homosexuality was a taboo subject and nobody told us anything about it. Must've been the same for you?'

'Well yes,' admitted Hilda. 'No-one told me anything about any sex come to that! I was caring for my disabled mother from when I was 12, you see.'

'That was tough on you – and a bit isolating I guess.'

Hilda's eyes filled at the unexpected sympathy. 'I didn't really have a choice.' She paused, remembering that difficult time.

'So when Jack came out, I was horrified.'

She sniffed, 'Then Martin left me and after that everything seemed to go wrong.'

Her tale unfolded, and Hilda and Linda sat there, until they could bear the cold no longer.

Hilda reflected as they walked back to their cars that

it had been really helpful talking to another mother in the same boat. Someone also with a lesbian daughter. She wished she'd been able to do this when Jack had come out, when she'd felt so isolated.

Furthermore, she resolved to return to the Blue Cross shop and see if Caroline would have her back after all this time.

Chapter 15 – Another Letter

Hilda had never expected to hear from Jack again. The letter arrived on a Saturday morning in April. She recognised Jack's handwriting on the envelope. It was large and angular, a mixture of upper and lower case letters in each word of the address. He left school at 16 having no qualifications, as his dyslexia had not been picked up there. A year after that he had left home, and gone to live with some fellow who owned the night club in Redditch.

Jack hadn't been doing so well at school before that. His parents hadn't known the reason for this until he came home crying when he was 14, with his shirt torn and a black eye, saying that he was being bullied. The children were calling him gay and yes, he knew he was gay, but they shouldn't do this. They constantly taunted him with name-calling, sniggering at him and writing notes to each other calling him a poof, a batty-boy and worse. The teachers didn't seem to notice and it had come to a head when some boys had beaten him up in the toilets. Hilda had been shocked initially at Jack's outburst, but as she put a cold compress on his eye, she reassured him indignantly that he was mistaken. Of course he wasn't gay. He would grow out of these feelings – it was just a phase. She remembered saying angrily that she wouldn't want him in the house if he was 'one of those sort.' Furthermore, his confusion was all his father's fault for not taking enough interest in him, or herself, for that matter.

She'd told Martin. He'd been similarly incredulous at the news and withdrew from the family all the more. She'd further blamed the divorce, which followed shortly after, on Jack's confession. She knew now that she had reacted unhelpfully for all of them. She understood that some of the anger and disbelief she'd felt towards Jack was confused with her feelings towards Martin and his behaviour.

Jack and she had parted on bad terms at that terrible time of her life. Martin left shortly after and she'd begun the divorce proceedings. She'd felt unable to cope with her grief. Not just with the fact that Martin had left her, but her inability to deal with the fact that Jack repeatedly insisted that he was gay at around the same time.

Jack knew she'd never accepted this fact and Hilda hadn't helped the situation by making pointed remarks at every opportunity. He couldn't have known that she cried herself to sleep every night. Once he'd stormed out and left home, she felt totally abandoned and as if she now lived in a different universe. His disclosure had hurt and shamed her almost more than Martin's betrayal.

Now she took his letter into the kitchen and put it on the side, as she filled and plugged in the kettle. Sooty shot in through the cat flap, mewing anxiously for his breakfast and rubbing himself against her legs. He was wet from the rain which had just started, so she shoved him away with her foot as she measured his dry food into a dish. She put his food on the floor, preoccupied with her memories of that difficult time years ago. Still the letter lay unopened.

'Oh dear, oh dear! What now I wonder,' she muttered under her breath, with sobs not far from her heart. She took a deep breath, picked up the envelope and ripped it open. Inside was a sheet of paper torn from a spiral-back notebook. She could barely decipher the unpunctuated scrawl pencilled on the lines.

'Hi Ma I gonna be a Plummer got a Prentiship left the club can I Cum home now luv Jack'.

There followed a mobile number.

He must be desperate for somewhere to live, thought

Hilda, if he's left the club. She felt her excitement mounting at the thought of seeing him and of there being a man in the house again, as indeed he'd be a man now. Could she bear it? She assumed he had no partner now. How would he behave? She thought for a moment that perhaps he had stopped all that nonsense about being gay. Then she chided herself for having such thoughts. She knew better now than to think that.

The steam from the over-boiled kettle misted her glasses and she made herself a cup of tea. She took that and the letter into the lounge. Sooty continued crunching his biscuits.

She considered how she should react. She was aware of her pleasure at the possibility of seeing Jack again and began to consider her options.

She was very lonely now, which was what she had feared all her life. She had been isolated as an adolescent when caring for her disabled mother after her father had left home. She had very few friends. Susan had stopped calling as regularly, even though, since the visit, they were on better terms than they had been. She still felt rather ashamed of her children, though to a lesser extent. It had been helpful talking to people with a different viewpoint.

She realised that if she refused to accept her children for who they were, they would reject her and she would be left alone. Although she feared the reactions of others, after talking to Linda it appeared that other people of her generation did not necessarily accept that being gay was wrong or a disgrace. Neither Caroline nor Linda did. This was also confirmed by the vicar who had called round a second time, for a further chat. She'd felt it was safe to confide in him. After all he didn't seem to share her view that her children, or even the entire family, would be damned in hell for eternity.

She had a choice: to accept her children's sexuality and behaviour as normal and brazen it out. But then people might laugh at her behind her back. She'd chosen so far not to confide in anybody else – not even to phone the Helpline, which the vicar had mentioned existed for families and friends of lesbian and gay children.

Or she could rant and rave and announce to anyone who would listen that she disapproved, but then she'd have to see people's shocked reactions. She was essentially a quiet withdrawn person, very private, so this would go against her nature. Of course she could refuse to go out and withdraw totally, like she had from the church and the shop. But she realised that she'd only be punishing herself to do that and would become intensely lonely. She was waiting to see if the Blue Cross Manager would have her back after such a long absence.

She could try phoning Martin again, but she quickly dismissed that idea with a shudder. She could still hear the floozy's laughter in the background from her last call. A sob caught in her throat.

Jack would have to come home. She couldn't see her own son homeless. He may have changed after all this time. She could do with a man about the house. He seemed to have got himself an apprenticeship and she should be encouraging him. She took a deep breath, picked up her phone and dialled his mobile.

Chapter 16 – Karen's thoughts

The dirty breakfast dishes were piled in the sink. Tom's football boots lay muddy in the middle of the rug. Time enough to sort those later. Karen sat knitting in the sunny chair by the window, her green crocheted shawl draped over the back, and her long blonde hair hanging over her eyes. The colour of the knitting would leave Sue unaware that it was a baby jacket. The white cat batted the purple wool it had been watching attentively as her needles clicked, but Karen was absorbed in her thoughts.

What would it be like to have a baby in the house again? What would the donor father be like? Would the baby look more like him than Sue? What would the neighbours say? She could imagine the prim and proper old couple down the road sniffing in disdain and tutting, as they had done when they saw her and Sue holding hands in the park. But then a baby often changes people, even if they would most likely see it as one born 'out of wedlock'. She surmised that the modern young couple who lodged next door to their house would not be bothered. They had eyes only for each other.

What would it be like to be one of a baby's two mums? She had coped well for the past eight years as a single mum. She and Sue had not long moved in together and she knew the other villagers were curious as to their relationship.

After Karen had adopted Tom, Linda her mum, had come up trumps when it came to helping her. The Adoption Agency had not been in the least worried by the fact that she was lesbian, but more concerned that she was single and would need support systems in place. So at the age of 32 she had moved back home and in fact had only recently moved away again to this cottage she rented with Sue, nearer Tom's school. Sue having her own baby was a quite different scenario, she guessed, and the neighbours would obviously be curious.

The needles were still clacking when Sue let herself in quietly and went straight to the bathroom, retching.

Chapter 17 – The Storm

The water, normally babbling in the stream below, had deepened its tone until it was almost a roar, so Karen knew that the water was rising rapidly.

It was mid-afternoon Sunday and she was in the deckchair by the back door knitting. She was thinking to catch an earlier patch of sunlight. Then the skies darkened without warning and the sun disappeared. Lightning flashed, followed immediately by a huge crash of thunder which cracked open the heavens above her. She looked up, startled, from her knitting. Alarmed, she stared at a threatening glow in the distance over the trees. It looked as if something was on fire. Could it be the farmer's barn beyond the woods? The garden gate was swinging on its hinges, creaking eerily and banging in the sudden wind. There was no rain, but suddenly with a roar like a huge chuffing steam engine the wind whipped up into a whirling frenzy, noisily scattering the loose leaves and snapping young shoots in the garden. Karen stood up and her long hair and skirt rose in turmoil. The deckchair hurtled off down the steps from the porch with a clatter. Clutching her knitting, she turned and pushed through the door to get back indoors.

As it banged behind her, she heard a low moan from the bathroom. Forgetting the storm and breathing heavily, she rushed upstairs, pushing open the bathroom door. Sue was on the floor, doubled up in pain.

'Oh no! What's happening?'

'I ... I think ... I'm losing ... the baby,' gasped Sue between sobs.

Karen knelt down beside her and rubbed her back as another clap of thunder shook the house.

'Oh, darling!' was all she could say. She gazed around desperately and grabbed her towel from the rail to put under her head. Then she noticed the blood oozing from between Sue's legs and reached for the other towel.

'I'll phone the doctor!' She felt in her pocket for her mobile, which she realised she'd left downstairs.

'I'm just getting my mobile. Stay there!' she ordered unnecessarily. She could feel sobs rising in her own throat as she took the stairs two at a time. All that they had gone through and now it was all for nothing! They'd been sure the pregnancy would go smoothly since the twelve weeks had passed and they'd even celebrated with a glass of wine last night.

Her mobile signal was dipping in and out because of the storm. Karen was trying not to panic and rushed upstairs again.

'A medic will be here soon,' she lied to comfort the sobbing Sue.

The whole house was creaking and shaking and they could hear rain drumming on the roof.

'I should never have tried this,' gasped Sue. 'It's not meant for us – it's because we're lesbian, isn't it?'

'Rubbish!' admonished Karen. 'If you'd stayed with Dave you might've got pregnant. Lots of people have miscarriages and it's nothing to do with being lesbian. We'll try again.'

'Don't want to after this,' gasped Sue, as another pain wracked her. 'But Tom – what time's he home?'

'He's playing with a friend, so not till later. It's all right,' she soothed Sue, rubbing her back.

'The nurse said just to take things easy and make yourself comfortable. I had to phone NHS direct. Can you sit up at all? We need to sit you on the loo really.'

The storm had died down when Karen's mobile rang later, although the stream had climbed out of its bed and was still rushing noisily through the lower garden.

'It's just the NHS nurse checking you are OK. They couldn't get here because of the storm – there are trees down between here and the clinic. But they will need you to get yourself checked by the doctor soon.'

Much later that evening when Tom was in bed, Sue and Karen sat quietly together. Sue was lying on the settee, the cramps had subsided and the huge blood clots had passed. Karen had squeezed in beside her head, which she had now cradled on her lap, stroking her forehead. They were saying nothing. Karen had shoved the baby knitting wool and needles down the side of the settee and had made sure she sat at that end.

'It's a bereavement,' sobbed Sue after a while. 'We've lost our baby. I've let us down,' and she wept again.

Sue continued to weep. Karen tried to comfort her, feeling helpless.

Later Sue's mobile rang, though Karen answered it.

'It's your mum.'

Sue shook her head, so Karen continued with the call.

'No, I'm sorry but she's not up to talking now, Hilda. Sadly, she's just had a miscarriage.'

Sue gasped and shrank into the settee. She stared wide-eyed as Karen continued the conversation, looking quizzically at her partner.

'Well yes. Didn't she tell you?'

Pause.

'Oh, about three months now.'

A longer pause this time.

'No, it's not Dave's. Look, we'll explain another time. I must look after Sue now. Yes, she'll be all right – really. I'll let you know.'

Pause.

'Yes of course I will. Goodbye Hilda.'

Karen clicked off the phone and faced Sue, her face thunderous.

'Well? You told me you'd tell her and you didn't! She knows now anyway.'

She got up and flounced into the kitchen. Sue sobbed quietly.

Chapter 18 – The Reconciliation

Jack travelled by bus to the house where he'd been brought up, feeling quite anxious. It had been 12 years since he'd been home after all the trouble with his parents. He'd moved away to work at a pub as a washer-up, until he was old enough to serve at the bar. Steve, the manager, had given him a room and one thing had led to another.

He could see nothing through the window of the bus, as it was fogged inside and pouring with rain outside, giving all the grey shapes along the road a misty appearance.

Jack got off the bus and walked the short distance up the hill to his mother's detached house, shivering as the rain slashed down on him unrelentingly and the wind gusted around. Nervous, wet from head to foot, he rang the bell, unsure of his reception. Hilda opened the door and he was relieved to see her face beaming. Behind him the bus pulled away up the hill and at his feet a soggy cat streaked past, desperate to get inside, but scarcely noticed by either mother or son. Hilda stepped back and the door blew wide, caught by a gust of wind.

Jack smiled sheepishly at her and commented as he stepped inside with his small bag, 'It's vile out there. I'm soaked! Waited ages for the bus.'

'Good to see you Jack,' managed Hilda, still smiling. 'You look frozen. I'll make us some tea.'

Jack stood just inside the door which he'd closed behind him, almost warily, shivering violently and dripping on the doormat and shiny parquet flooring. 'I need a towel!'

He shook his shock of black hair violently, like a dog, the spray going everywhere. He wrapped his arms around himself, as Hilda took a step back to avoid getting wet. She turned and hurried into the kitchen.

'Take your shoes off. There's a towel in the airing cupboard,' she instructed over her shoulder, as she busied with the kettle.

Jack kicked off his trainers and took the stairs two at a time. He came back down almost immediately, rubbing his head vigorously on a worn towel. His trousers and jacket were beginning to steam. Hilda looked him up and down.

'Didn't you bring any other clothes?' she asked as she poured the boiling water on the tea.

'Yes, of course, here in my bag,' He stooped and unzipped the bulging black 'Head' bag he'd dropped on the doormat as he came in.

'Don't undress there!' expostulated Hilda, 'Go up to your room!' She laughed hollowly, 'It's still in the same place!'

'Thanks, Ma.'

Jack shot her a grateful look and galloped upstairs again to his old room at the front of the house. Everything here was as he remembered it and he smiled at the faded posters of Kylie Minogue and Prince Harry above the single bed with the Superman duvet cover. He glanced out of the window at the familiar landscape, and saw that the rain was beginning to slacken. The old Norman church was still there obviously, but there was now an estate of pretentious red-brick houses in what had been a field of black and white cows ten years before. He could see that the old farm building beyond, just visible through the bare trees, was now a health and fitness gym.

He smiled at himself in the mirror and knew that his frame had thickened and despite his small stature he was a handsome man now, with a brush of black moustache on his upper lip.

Jack dumped his sodden clothing in the bathroom

across the landing and hurried downstairs again in a pair of black jeans and a grey sweatshirt. Hilda was waiting with the tea tray in the lounge. He noted that the furniture was still the same, with the writing bureau and the three piece chintz suite in their place. The black cat sat washing in front of the warm log fire Hilda had lit earlier. It looked up briefly, but ignored Jack, not knowing him, and carried on washing. Jack noticed it had only one eye.

'Nothing's changed, except for the cat. What's his name?'

'Sooty,' said Hilda smiling and settled herself at one end of the settee. 'Well, what's your news?'

'Well,' said Jack in the same tone of voice, as he took the proffered cup and sat down on the other end of the settee. He chose his words carefully.

'I worked with Steve for years and had lodgings with him, but when the job ended I had to move out.'

'So your relationship broke up too,' said his mother shrewdly. 'That must've been hard.'

Jack looked up, surprised that she had acknowledged his relationship and at her uncharacteristic sympathetic tone of voice.

'I didn't expect you to say that – but yes.'

He paused, the feelings churning inside him. He continued stiffly in a low voice,

'Sue called me. She said you had changed, that's why I thought I could come back and we could perhaps try again.'

'Indeed Jack, I have changed. I'm trying to understand more now,' acknowledged Hilda, with some difficulty.

'I'm sorry it's been so hard for you. I thought you would grow out of it. I had no idea!'

She sighed and continued,

'You see, you have to understand that I knew nothing about homosexuality.'

Jack winced and glowered at the old-fashioned word.

'I don't really know much more now. Only from talking to Linda – Karen's mum – oh, and the new vicar who explained things.'

Jack stiffened as he remembered what had happened a few years back with the previous incumbent, matters of which Hilda remained unaware.

Hilda continued, 'You see it wasn't talked about in my generation and my mother never told me anything – she couldn't. I was never prepared for life and I grew up very sheltered from the real world out there. I couldn't mix with the other teenagers, once ...' her voice faltered slightly, 'after the accident that is. I was only 12.'

Jack nodded. He was beginning to understand his mother's rigid views. Sue was right. Talking to Karen's mum seemed to have moved her on, however. He relaxed into the settee, contemplating the one-eyed cat and the fire. He clicked his fingers.

'He came from the cat rescue like that. I couldn't cope with a kitten flying around the walls!'

Jack was aware of his mother looking sideways at him, seemingly with pleasure and pride, as Sooty got up and wandered over to him to have its ears scratched. He wondered if she realised how it took a lot of desperation and courage for him to have come home again after the things that had been said so many years ago. He wondered if she would acknowledge this.

'Well, what's it like to be home then?' she said eventually.

Jack laughed, 'Good, but different! Steve and I lived in a bit of a tip really. The place was a mess always, as we were both so busy. He was always going out. But I didn't know he was playing around with other guys. People he met off the internet. Idiot. That took up his time too.'

His laughter turned bitter, but he was surprised by her reply.

'I am so sorry,' she said gently with a sigh. 'It hurts doesn't it? I guess it's the same, whether it's a man or a woman. You love them and they deceive you.'

'Well, yes and no,' explained Jack, turning towards her at the other end of the settee. 'The difference with being gay is that you can't show your affection in public – like holding hands even, walking down the street. People stare and make comments – or worse. It can be downright dangerous in some areas of town. I can't talk about my boyfriend – or couldn't anyway – to some people. I have to watch what I say. '

'I hadn't thought of that,' said Hilda.

'And people who are gay, like me, know that they are different, and we don't fit in somehow. We're not as good as everyone else and feel all wrong. I feel less ...' He struggled to find the right word, 'less worthy somehow!'

He scowled into the fire and Sooty moved away towards Hilda. Jack noticed that she seemed affected as the cat jumped on her lap.

'You are not unworthy to me, Jack,' she said stoutly. 'I can see you are a fine young man and people are wrong to judge you by your relationships. I am sorry that we did.'

It was Jack's turn to be moved and he angrily brushed

away a tear from his eyes. It was good to be home, despite everything, and he felt more comfortable by the minute.

'You don't know how hard it was for me when I came out to you and Dad,' he said. 'And with those kids at school who never let up. Then you went on at me. That's why I had to leave.'

'Have you spoken to … your Dad?' enquired Hilda, after a pregnant pause. Jack glanced at her mentioning the forbidden name. There was another pause, then he spoke gruffly.

'Yes, I've been seeing him most weeks since I left home. He comes into the bar at the Knave on Tuesdays with Shelley.'

Jack noticed that his mother stiffened, but said nothing. So he continued,

'It was easier to talk to him because he didn't judge me all the time. I suppose he couldn't criticise, because he'd done wrong by leaving us all.'

Hilda did cry then and the cat jumped off her lap.

'I tried so much, but I didn't get any of it right did I?' she sobbed. 'I'm so sorry – it must have been so hard for you. And you were so young.'

Jack sat still and let her cry, knowing that she didn't

like to be comforted. There were few hugs from her as children, but they had always gone to their father who was more openly affectionate.

'You were good enough Ma,' said Jack gruffly. 'It can't have been easy and I was a bit of a tearaway. It's not your fault we are both gay.'

'No, I know that now,' sniffed Hilda drying her eyes. 'But I did blame your Dad and me. Then we broke up of course.'

Jack snorted, 'I was gay before that. And the kids at school made sure I knew!'

He remembered the time they had beaten him up in the toilets and he had come home to a less than helpful welcome from his parents. He glanced at his mother and knew she remembered also from the uneasy way she changed her position on the settee, turning away from him slightly and dabbing at her eyes.

After a while, Hilda said, 'So, what now?'

Jack looked at her square in the face as he said,

'I want to come home, Ma. I've no-where else to stay and I've got no job now. I thought I might try for an apprenticeship with someone, or look for bar work here. I wasn't quite honest when I wrote that note, but I want a new start. I could try the college for a plumbing course or something.'

'Well, we could give it another go,' said Hilda warmly. 'I could do with a man about the place. Everywhere needs decorating and I struggle now to keep the garden going.'

'Yes, I could help a bit about the place,' said Jack reluctantly. He shifted uneasily and glanced around at the woodchip wallpaper and dull paintwork.

'Well that's settled then,' said Hilda comfortably and Sooty jumped back on her lap.

Chapter 19 – Settling in

Hilda was baking a cake. Jack could hear her sniffing as she weighed and poured. Through the open hatch between the two rooms he could smell peppermint essence as she counted aloud the drops into the mixture, 'one, two, three, four.'

The heat from the kitchen drifted through into the living room, where Jack had settled comfortably into the settee. All was quiet except for Mum's clattering in the kitchen. Jack was supposed to be clearing the ashes from the grate and laying the fire ready for the evening, but he thought he would sit and read the paper first. He had a flashback to his Dad doing the same, many years before, with Mum nagging him. The cat, confident with him now, was curled up asleep on his lap. He reflected how different life was here, compared to the chaotic flat above the pub.

His mother's grey leather handbag was propped against the wing-back chair. He knew it contained her shabby red leather purse; her key for the disabled toilets which she had never returned after Gran had died some years ago, and some tissues for her constantly dripping nose. He'd seen her put a map of Bromsgrove in there last night, which had puzzled him slightly as he didn't know that Hilda had met Linda, Karen's mother, at Hanbury Hall some weeks earlier. He'd also spotted his own letter in there when she'd tipped all the contents onto the table the evening before, searching for her favourite pen. The lip-salve had rolled onto the floor and the new mobile she was still struggling to use had winked at him from the polished surface. The letter was the one he'd written to his mother a few weeks before when his relationship with Steve had ended and he'd asked to come home. He'd been surprised to see that his mother now carried a pocket mirror too, given that traditionally she'd she spent very little time or effort on her appearance.

He jumped when the mobile rang and Sooty leapt off his lap with a growl, the cat's claws catching his leg.

'Answer that will you, dear,' called his mother from the kitchen, as he heard her open the oven door and then slam it.

It was Susan.

'Oh, hi Sue … Yes, much better … She's baking a cake, but I'll take her the phone …'

He carried on talking as he handed it through the hatch to Hilda, who was wiping her hands down her apron.

'Yes, next term, I hope. Bye.'

He gave the phone to his Mother and thought about the plumbing course he was to take. It was a daunting prospect to be training again at his age, but he knew it was a better path to take than the pub work.

He knelt down by the fire and began to rake out the ashes. His mother, holding the small phone awkwardly with her floury hands, talked to his sister.

Chapter 20 – The Wedding

Hilda had gone to the vicar in great excitement to tell him about Susan and Karen getting married. She expected that she, or they, would book the church for the wedding in a few weeks time. Luke had expressed real pleasure that they were getting married, and that she'd come to tell him about it. The conversation however, turned to embarrassment when she'd asked about a church ceremony. He flushed and pursed his lips, as if wanting to say something different.

'Hilda, I'm afraid the Anglican Church does not allow same-sex marriages on its premises.'

She had stared at him in disbelief and protested,

'But it's legal now! And my children were baptised. In the church here in fact. They both sang in the choir and Jack was a bell-ringer.'

'I know, and it puts me in a difficult position. But the Church of England doesn't recognise same-sex marriage, because of some arguments about Biblical teachings. A lot of the clergy are still arguing about it. The government actually made it law that people couldn't get married in church, because of all the disunity. You see, it's the Established Church. The decision continues to cause controversy, of course. It is, however, expressly forbidden in Canon Law for me or any clergyman to marry same-sex couples. Some of us are campaigning against this. But I can't take the wedding – I'm so sorry!'

He had looked visibly distressed as he spoke.

Hilda remembered her shock and dismay at his words. She had realised, however, that her anger could be more usefully directed towards the church, rather than the members of her own family.

So she now stood proudly in the front row of the hall at the Hilton Hotel, as her daughter and Karen walked up the aisle between the rows of seats in the wedding room. They had decided that, as they were both independent of family, there would be no 'giving away' nonsense. Both brides wore cream – Sue in a long full skirt and Karen in trousers, but they had matching jackets and pink rose buttonholes. Sue's bump was scarcely visible in her chunky frame.

Tom had refused to be pushed into the role of page boy, but stood in his new leather jacket and smart trousers, sullen with embarrassment, at Hilda's side. He had a toy car in his pocket with which he fidgeted. He had been promised a Game Boy later, if he behaved. Linda was the other side of him. The two women from time to time smiled at each other over his head.

Martin and Shelley were on the opposite side of the aisle, as was Jack with his new partner, a handsome fine-featured man of Asian appearance. Hilda reflected on her own wedding many years before, when protocol had to be strictly observed: groom's family on the right, bride's family on the left. Nowadays, the diversity within families was so wide-ranging, with the recognition of blended families, as well as gay families: anything was possible.

Hilda reflected on how she herself had changed over the last year and how much better life had become since she'd dared to accept her children for who they really were. She felt much closer to both of them and considered both Linda and Karen to be part of her extended new family. She'd realised that many of her friends had different families too, with step-children and foster children, and that they were all more relaxed with her because she'd come to terms with her situation. She could now even mention Martin's name in conversation with their children.

After thinking about it, she was more open to understanding her own part in the marriage breakup. She seemed to have healed somewhat from the deep hurt she had felt at their father's betrayal. She was even pleased that he'd been able to continue the relationship with both their children.

Hilda struggled however, to forgive Shelley and refused any eye contact with her. It was, nevertheless, difficult for her to completely ignore the smiling baby boy, held proudly in the younger woman's arms.

Sue's new baby was due in six months, following her successful pregnancy after the earlier miscarriage and Hilda was looking forward to this grandchild with excitement. She was pleased to be a second grandma to Tom, and to know that she was becoming important in his life too. She was even able to look with pleasure at the photos of her friends' grandchildren when she met up with them.

Hilda felt very proud of Jack's courage in coming out in difficult circumstances so young. She liked his new partner, Ahmed, whom in fact she had known for years as one of Jack's school contemporaries. He was the son of the Patels who ran the shop in the village. She and they had since talked together; about the challenges and prejudices they had faced in themselves, before feeling able to accept their gay sons. They all felt proud of them now.

Altogether, everyone was happier. She wouldn't want her family to be any different now. She scarcely remembered how she had felt when the children first came out. She knew she was a different person; in future she wouldn't care what the villagers chose to gossip about.

Appendix

Dates in LGBT history significant to this story:

World Health Organisation removed 'ego-dystonic homosexuality' from the Diagnostic and Statistic Manual of mental disorders. 1987

Under Prime Minister Margaret Thatcher, Section 28, of the Local Government Act prevents the 'promotion' of homosexuality by local authorities, and reference is made to 'Pretended families.'

1988

Equal rights are granted to same-sex couples applying for Adoption.

2002

Repeal of Section 28 of the Local Government Act.

2003

Civil Partnership Act passed in November giving same-sex couples the same rights and responsibilities as married heterosexual couples.

2004

Government announces that the first civil partnerships for same sex couples can be registered on 5 December, taking effect from 21 December 2005 (after the 15 day waiting period).

Same-sex Marriage Act.

2014

If you are affected by any of the issues discussed in this book, then you can contact any of these organisations for support:

Families and Friends of Lesbians and Gays
(www.fflag.org.uk)

Changing Attitude
(www.changingattitude.org.uk)

Lesbian and Gay Christian Movement
(www.lgcm.org.uk)

PACT
(www.pactcharity.org)

Adoption UK
(www.adoptionuk.org)

Glossary

IUI: Intrauterine insemination

IVF: In vitro fertilisation

GCHQ: Government Communications Headquarters

AIDS: Acquired Immune Deficiency Syndrome

ABOUT THE AUTHOR

Margaret Evans has supported parents of lesbian, gay, bisexual and trans (LGBT) children, in association with FFLAG. She was formerly a teacher, accredited counsellor and trainer. She has researched couple-counsellors' perceptions of LGB people and has published academic and other articles. She has published poems, but this is her first foray into fiction.

41222246R00069

Made in the USA
Charleston, SC
26 April 2015